GHOSTS
OF THE SKIES

Aviation in the Second World War

PHILIP MAKANNA

CHRONICLE BOOKS
SAN FRANCISCO

Fifty years have passed.

These are reflections of a time gone by.

They are for Nicholas.

Copyright © 1995 by Philip Makanna

Printed in Hong Kong.

Library of Congress Cataloging-in-Publication Data:

Makanna, Philip, 1940-
    Ghosts of the Skies: Aviation in the Second World War/Philip
  Makanna.
      p. cm.
      Includes index.
      ISBN 0-8118-0742-8
      1. Airplanes, Military—Pictorial works. 2. World War, 1939-1945—
  Equipment. I. Title
  UG1240. M342 1995
358. 4 ' 009044—dc20   94-39453
                                   CIP

Design: Morla Design, Inc., San Francisco, CA

Distributed in Canada by Raincoast Books
8680 Cambie Street
Vancouver, BC V6P 6M9

10 9 8 7 6 5 4 3 2 1

Chronicle Books
275 Fifth Street
San Francisco, CA 94103

CONTENTS

—

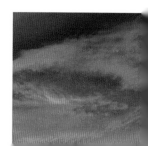

"How horrible, fantastic, incredible it is that we should be digging trenches and trying on gas masks here because of a quarrel in a far-away country between people of whom we know nothing."

Neville Chamberlain, radio broadcast concerning Hitler's threatened invasion of Czechoslovakia, September 27, 1938

Preface

The World War II aircraft pictured in this book are specters of time past. With each passing day, the great planes—the Mustangs and the Flying Fortresses, the Mosquitoes and the Spitfires—begin to resemble mythical beasts, their purposes and their stories receding into the mists. The war's vast air armadas and epic battles flicker indistinctly in our memories as they fade gradually and inexorably from the world's stage.

Heralded as symbols of industrial might, hundreds of thousands of aircraft were built during the war. Only a restored handful remain, curiosities and mementos of a great historical event. The aircraft featured here have been rescued from the scrap heap and refurbished after long hours of work. They are not flown often, for they are survivors, and the risk of loss is great. They are phantoms, obsolete and ancient, but they are also loud and powerful and fast. In flight, they are simply thrilling to watch.

Lost in time, the thundering bombers, the twisting fighters, the chaos of combat, and the stab of mortal fear remain in the memories of the crews who flew these aircraft. Like the machines themselves, the pilots and bombardiers, the navigators and gunners, grow fragile, their thoughts shadowed by the passing years.

Their tales have been told countless times: the numbing fatigue of long hours and high altitude; the sheer terror of slashing machine-gun attacks against a bomber stream; the mindless boredom of military duties; the thankful release of tension when a mission was completed—pale words to express intense emotions. We cannot know every combatant's inner story: what it was really like; how they felt; what they were before battle—and after. Those mysteries remain.

The air crews were young to be in command of such power. Like the machines they flew, they were instruments of destruction, yet in the performance of their duties they often exhibited the highest human ideals of courage, self-sacrifice, and tenacity. For good or for evil, the fliers were among the best of their generation.

Fifty years after, we have precious little to memorialize the war: several restored aircraft, a clutch of words from those who fought, and a few images, from the past and the present. Yet taken together, the pieces tell a compelling story.

Photographer Philip Makanna has gathered selected bits of history, combined them with his own contemporary photos, and produced a startling image of aircraft at war. Linking the past with the present, this is Makanna's homage to a time he never knew, to the aircraft of World War II and to their crews.

As a young boy in the late 1940s, Makanna often heard tales of air combat in World War II. The stories were told by the men who had flown the bombers and the fighters in history's most destructive conflict. Even then, only short years after the war, the details were beginning to blur, but the memories and the storytellers still had the power to stir a young boy's fantasies. Intrigued by what he heard and perpetually fascinated by the dream of flight, Makanna longed to be a pilot. His eyes proved not good enough, so he followed other interests, becoming a painter, a filmmaker, and eventually a photographer.

In the course of an assignment in Nevada, in 1974, he came face-to-face with his childhood dreams. During the Reno Air Races, a group of pilots from the Confederate Air Force reenacted the 1941 attack on Pearl Harbor. On that day, there were Zeros over the sagebrush, the rumble of big radial engines, a P-40 Warhawk painted with the jaws of death.

Sparked by that chance encounter, Makanna became a specialist in the photography of World War II aircraft. In locations throughout the world he has used his camera to capture the essence of these intriguing machines. Over the past twenty years, he has published two books of aircraft photographs and a continuing series of calendars, all entitled *Ghosts*.

This latest book is divided into four parts: Earth, Water, Air, and Fire, the elements comprising the very essence of existence according to ancient and medieval thinkers. The four sections trace a broadly defined sequence of wartime events and aviation development.

The first chapter, Earth, sketches the beginning of hostilities and the Battle of Britain—the attack upon the land and the defense of the island nation. Next is the ocean war, which in the Pacific saw the creation of the great aircraft carrier battle groups. Third is Air. It is about flight itself and is illustrated by a wide variety of aircraft that fought in every part of the world, from the Arctic to the Sahara. Fire completes the commemoration, for these are, after all, combat aircraft, designed to deliver destruction.

Today, these old warriors—the planes and the crews—no longer breathe fire. All seem to appreciate the allurements of peace and are content simply to be flying. They are ghosts indeed. In flight, they remind us not of their destructive purpose but of the ingenuity, courage, and cooperative efforts that gave them form and launched them into the skies.   *–Charles Robbins*

"England has been offered a choice between war and shame.

She has chosen shame and will get war."

Winston Churchill, speech in the British House of Commons concerning the Munich agreement, September, 1938

earth

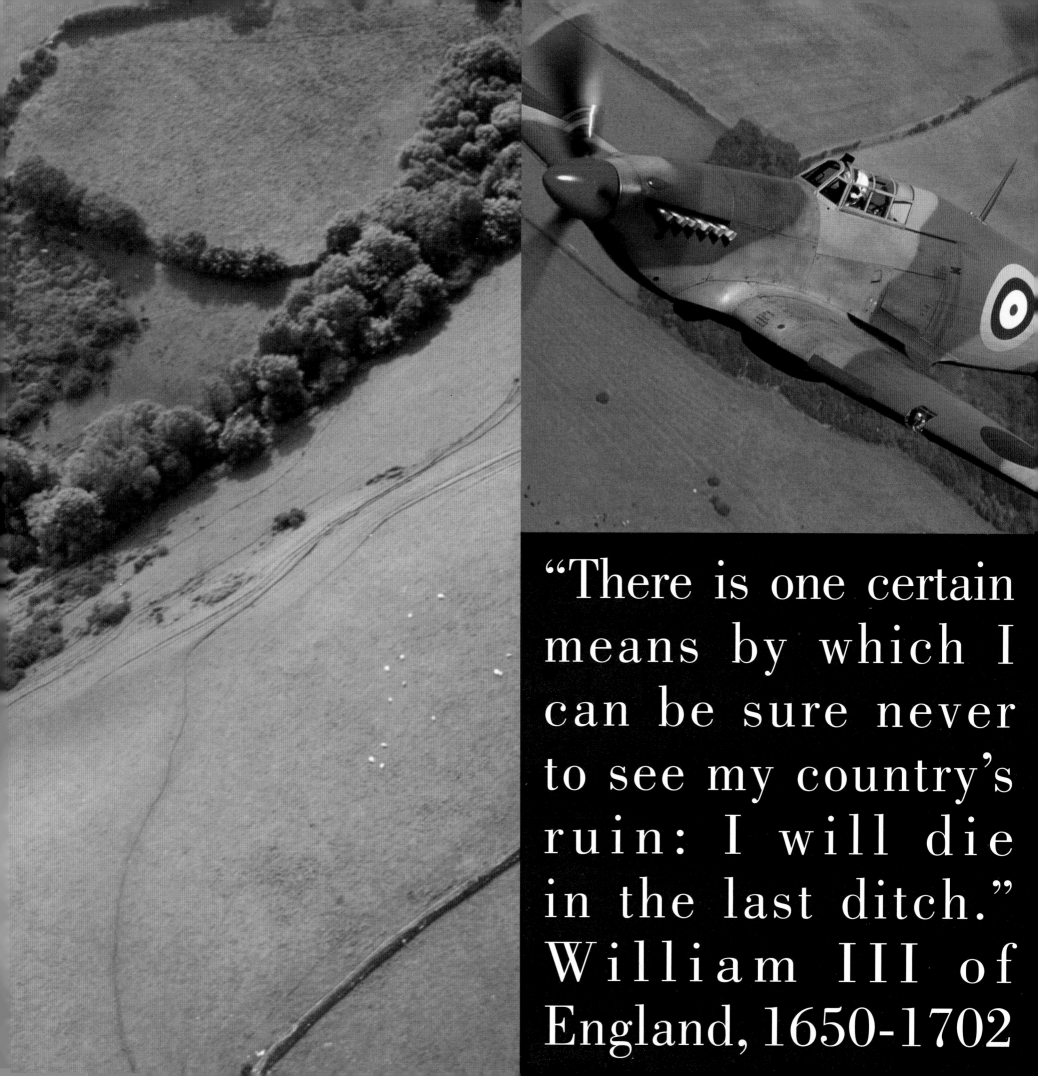

"There is one certain means by which I can be sure never to see my country's ruin: I will die in the last ditch." William III of England, 1650-1702

World War II Aerial Ace

Gloster "Gladiator" Mk. II

Last of the Royal Air Force's biplane fighters, the Gladiator had several modern touches such as an enclosed cockpit and heavy firepower, features that pointed the way to future developments in the monoplane fighter. Although obsolete, Gladiators operated in France, Norway, and Malta during the war's early months.

Hawker "Hind"

A pre-war bomber, the Hind was used primarily as a trainer by the British during World War II. The Hind was the last in a long series of Hawker aircraft stretching back to the 1920s.

"Mankind has grown strong in eternal struggles and it will only perish through eternal peace."

Adolf Hitler, *Mein Kampf*, 1924

A Nazi seaplane base near
the English Channel, 1939

"Silent, mournful, abandoned, broken, Czechoslovakia recedes into darkness. . . . Do not suppose that this

is the end. This is only the beginning."

Winston Churchill, speech in the House of Commons concerning the Munich agreement, October 5, 1938

Fairey "Swordfish" Mk. II,
Dover, England

Appropriately nicknamed the
Stringbag, Fairey's biplane was
out-of-date before the war began,
yet it served throughout the conflict. Swordfish saw important
service in many Fleet Air Arm
actions, including the sinking of
the German battleship *Bismarck*
and the destruction of the Italian
fleet at Taranto.

Fairey "Swordfish" Mk. II,
aboard HMS *Tracker*

Apparently outmoded at the
beginning of the war, the
Ju52 nevertheless remained
Germany's primary aircraft for
airborne assault and supply.

"This morning the British Ambassador in Berlin handed the German government a final note stating that

unless we heard from them by eleven o'clock that they were prepared at once to withdraw their troops from

Poland, a state of war would exist between us. I have to tell you now that no such undertaking has been

received and that consequently this country is at war with Germany."

Neville Chamberlain, radio broadcast, September 3, 1939

Messerschmitt Me208/Nord 1101

A variant of the more numerous Me108, the Nord was designed as a Luftwaffe communications and command aircraft.

"Has the last word been spoken? Must hope be abandoned? Is our defeat complete? No! France is not

alone! She is not alone! She is not alone! Whatever happens, the flame of French resistance must not

and will not be extinguished."

Charles de Gaulle, *"L'Appel du 18 Juin,"* BBC radio broadcast to the French people from London, June 18, 1940

Messerschmitt Me108/Nord
1002 "Taifun"

The Luftwaffe's main communication aircraft, the Taifun,
with its metal construction,
was a forerunner of the famous
Messerschmitt Bf109.

Fieseler "Storch" in front of the
Arsenal, Berlin, February 17, 1939

"... behind us, behind the armies and fleets of

Britain and France, gather a group of shattered

States and bludgeoned races: the Czechs, the Poles,

the Norwegians, the Danes, the Dutch, the Belgians,

upon all of whom the long night of barbarism will

descend, unbroken even by a star of hope."

Winston Churchill, radio broadcast, London, May 19, 1940

Fieseler Fi.156D "Storch"

This STOL (Short Take-Off and
Landing) aircraft was a mainstay
of Luftwaffe reconnaissance and
communication operations. It
was flown by Otto Skorzeny in
the 1943 rescue of Mussolini,
who had been captured by Italian
partisans and held prisoner in
the Apennine mountains.

Hitler before the Reichstag
after completion of the "union"
with Austria

"The defense of southern England will last four days and the

Royal Air Force four weeks. We can guarantee invasion for the

Führer within a month."

Hermann Goering, Reichsmarschall, Nazi Germany, at a Luftwaffe
chiefs-of-staff meeting at Karinhall, July 11, 1940

Symbol of Britain's defiance
during the Battle of Britain,
the Spitfire was designed in the
1930s. Updated models kept
the Spitfire in the forefront of
fighter development. It was the
only Allied fighter in production
at the beginning of the war
and at its end.

Hawker "Hurricane" Mk. XIIa

Hurricanes were the most numerous British fighter of the Battle
of Britain. They destroyed more
enemy aircraft than all other
defensive systems combined.
As the war progressed and more
advanced fighters appeared, the
Hurricane was increasingly used
in the anti-tank and ground
attack role.

British Prime Minister Winston Churchill

"... the battle of France is over. The Battle of Britain is about to begin. Upon this battle depends

the survival of Christian civilization. If we fail, then the whole world, including the United States,

including all that we have known and cared for, will sink into the abyss of a new Dark Age. Let

us therefore brace ourselves to our duties, and so bear ourselves that, if the British Empire and its

Commonwealth last for a thousand years, men will still say, 'This was their finest hour.'"

Winston Churchill, speech in the House of Commons, June 18, 1940

Messerschmitt Bf109G-2 Trop

The main Luftwaffe fighter
throughout World War II, the
109 was fast and robust.
The highest-scoring ace in the
war, Major Erich Hartmann
(352 victories) flew a 109.

"From Britain I now hear only a single cry . . . that . . . the

war must go on. It almost causes me pain to think that I

should have been selected by Fate to deal the final blow."

Adolf Hitler, Der Führer, speech before the German Reichstag,
July 19, 1940

Adolf Hitler addressing a Nazi
Party rally at Nuremberg

"Thousands of you in this country have had to leave your homes and be separated

from your fathers and mothers. My sister, Margaret Rose, and I feel so much for

you, as we know from experience what it means to be away from those we love most

of all. To you, living in new surroundings, we send a message of true sympathy,

and at the same time we would love to thank the kind people who have welcomed

you to their homes in the country. When peace comes, remember, it will be for us,

the children of today to make the world of tomorrow a better and happier place.

My sister is by my side, and we are both going to say good night to you. Come on,

Margaret. Good night, children. Good night and good luck to you all."

Princess Elizabeth, aged fourteen, speaks by radio to the children of London who
have been separated from their families, evacuated from their homes, and sent to live
in the country, October 13, 1940

Children being evacuated
from London, June 13, 1940

Heinkel He111 (C.A.S.A. 2111)

A Heinkel 111 over London,
September 7, 1940

Used extensively as a bomber
early in the war, the 111 was the
Luftwaffe's primary bomber. It
was vulnerable to fighter attack
and eventually was relegated to
transport work.

Junkers Ju87 "Stuka" (Replica)

"We shall go on to the end, we shall fight in France,

we shall fight on the seas and oceans, we shall fight

with growing confidence and growing strength in the

air, we shall defend our Island, whatever the cost

may be, we shall fight on the beaches, we shall fight

on the landing grounds, we shall fight in the fields

and in the streets, we shall fight in the hills; we shall

never surrender."

Winston Churchill, speech in the House of Commons after
the defeat at Dunkirk, June 4, 1940

Junkers Ju87 "Stuka"

The symbol of Blitzkrieg, the Stuka was a weapon of terror early in the war. However, its low speed and lack of maneuverability meant it could only be used in areas of Luftwaffe air superiority.

London, Fire Storm, December 29, 1940

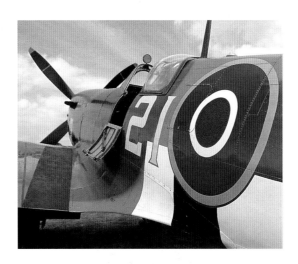

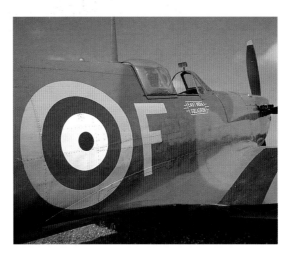

Supermarine "Spitfire" Mk. IX

Supermarine "Spitfire" Mk. IXe

Supermarine "Spitfire" Mk. Vc

Supermarine "Spitfire" Mk. XIV

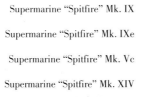

"We were young fighter pilots, scarcely schoolboys. Some of us had our homes within sight of our

airfields. I often used to fly to Portsmouth in the Battle of Britain and look down on my family home. It

was a very personal thing. You got into your aeroplane and felt the fears that everybody feels when going

off to fight. Overpowering all of that was this feeling that if you and all your chaps didn't do your

damnedest on every operation that you took off on, then all these Germans were going to be flooding over

your country, over your homes, destroying everything that you thought was worth preserving."

Wing Commander Roland P. Beaumont

"The hour destined by Fate is sounding for us. The hour of irrevocable decision has come. A declaration

of war has been handed to the ambassadors of Great Britain and France. Italian people, rush to arms

and show your tenacity, your courage, your valor!"

Benito Mussolini, (self-appointed) Supreme Commander of the Italian Armed Forces, national broadcast from the balcony of the Palazzo Venezia, June 10, 1940

Hitler and Mussolini
on maneuvers

Bristol "Blenheim" Mk. IVT

Blenheim crew touching bald pate for good luck

"The truth is that the village is not doing so badly. Men still live by net and plough, by fishing and fowling,

by the soil and the sea. The Brent geese still sit on the mudbanks at night, cronking in their thousands.

Overhead the bombers roar, searchlights pattern the sky with the fantastically beautiful geometry of war.

Guns thump and thud. Bombs have fallen on the village. Six of them fell among the oyster sheds, two in

the high street and one rattled the windows of the Fisherman's Club with a terrifying blast. But not a man

in all the mixed company in that little bar, where stuffed ducks gaze glassily, upset his beer."

J. Wentworth Day, "An East Coast Village in War Time," from *Country Life*, May 3, 1941

British soldier guarding fallen Bf109,
October 25, 1940

Messerschmitt Bf109G-2 Trop

Supermarine
"Spitfire" Mk. IXb

"This is no war of chieftains or of princes, of dynasties or national ambition. This is a war of peoples and of causes. There are vast numbers, not only in this Island, but in every land, who will render faithful service in this war, but whose names will never be known, whose deeds will never be recorded. This is a war of the unknown warriors; let all strive without failing in faith or in duty, and the dark curse of Hitler will be lifted from our age."

Winston Churchill, radio broadcast, London, July 14, 1940

Royal Air Force pilot,
Duxford, England, 1940

Squadron Leader
Douglas R.S. Bader,
Duxford, England,
September 26, 1940

Hawker "Hurricane" Mk. IIc

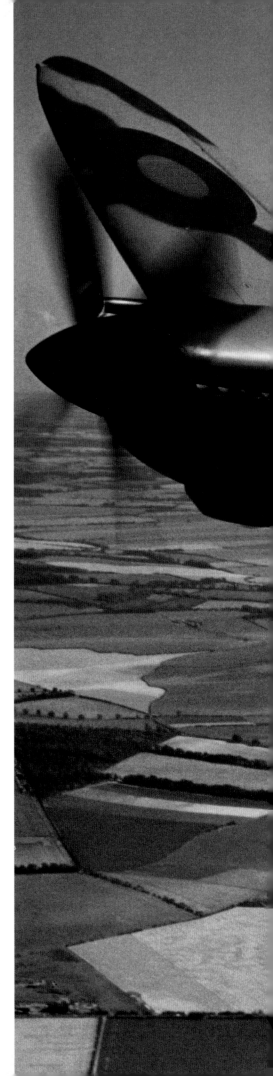

"The gratitude of every home in our Island, in our Empire, and indeed throughout the world, . . .

goes out to the British airmen who, undaunted by odds, unwearied in their constant challenge and

mortal danger, are turning the tide of the World War by their prowess and by their devotion. Never

in the field of human conflict was so much owed by so many to so few."

Winston Churchill, speech in the House of Commons on the role of the RAF in the Battle of Britain, August 20, 1940

RAF pilots, 19th Squadron, Duxford, England, 1940

Supermarine "Spitfire" Mk. IXb and Supermarine "Spitfire" Mk. IXe

water

"If it is necessary to fight, in the first six months to a year of war against the United States and England I will run wild. I will show you an uninterrupted succession of victories. But I must also tell you that if the war be prolonged for two or three years I have no confidence in our ultimate victory." Admiral Isoroku Yamamoto, Commander in Chief, Imperial Navy, to Emperor Hirohito prior to the Japanese attack on Pearl Harbor

"Once I prophesied that this generation of Americans had a rendezvous with destiny. That prophecy comes true. To us, much is given; more is expected. This generation will 'nobly save or meanly lose the last best hope on earth.' "

Franklin D. Roosevelt, annual message to Congress, January 4, 1939

Atlantic Ocean; American aircraft carrier en route to North Africa, November, 1942

Grumman F3F-2

Fairey "Firefly" Mk. 5 over the cliffs of Dover

"To make a people great one must thrust them into battle, even if you have to boot them

in the pants. . . . If we do not take advantage of this occasion to pit our Navy against

the French and British forces, what is the use of building 600,000 tons of warships?"

Benito Mussolini to King Victor Emmanuel III of Italy, May 13, 1940

A Vought-Sikorsky OS2U
"Kingfisher" is catapulted from
the deck of the USS *Texas* during
operations in the Mediterranean.

"What does the world think?

I do not care

Nor for my life

For I am the sword of my Emperor."

Admiral Isoroku Yamamoto, Commander in Chief,
Imperial Navy, December 7, 1941

Japanese pilot

Mitsubishi A6M5-52 "Zero"

Master of the air in Asia and the
Pacific until the Battle of Midway
(June 1942), this famous
Japanese fighter astounded the
Allies at the beginning of the war.
Highly maneuverable, it was also
fragile and lightly armed.

"We, by grace of Heaven, Emperor of Japan, seated on the throne of a line unbroken for ages eternal,

enjoin upon you, our loyal and brave subjects: We hereby declare war on the United States of America

and the British Empire."

Emperor Hirohito, formal declaration of war, Tokyo, December 7, 1941

Inside a Japanese bomber

"As I [assumed that I] was going to die, I decided I would take the enemy with me. I swung the bomber over hard and headed directly for him. The pilot appeared startled at my maneuver and fled. I asked myself: 'Is this what is called war?'"

Chief Flight Petty Officer Juzo Mori, Pearl Harbor, December 7, 1941

Two Nakajima B5N "Kates" (Replicas)

Front-line Japanese torpedo bomber early in the war, the Kate was the third plane in the successful triad (including the Zero and Val) that marked Japanese military success during the early stages of the war.

Three Aichi D3A "Vals" (Replicas)

Japan's dive-bomber early in the war, the Val led bombing attacks at Pearl Harbor. Later in the war, it was effective only as a kamikaze.

"Tora . . . Tora . . . Tora . . ." (*"Tiger . . . Tiger . . . Tiger . . ."*)

Commander Mitsuo Fuchida, informing the Imperial Japanese Fleet that the surprise
attack on Pearl Harbor was successful, December 7, 1941

"*Yesterday, December 7, 1941—a date which will live in infamy—the United States of America was suddenly and deliberately attacked by naval and air forces of the Empire of Japan. No matter how long it may take us to overcome this premeditated invasion, the American people, in their righteous might, will win through to absolute victory.*"

Franklin D. Roosevelt, message to Congress asking for Declaration of the Existence of War between the United States and Japan, December 8, 1941

Grumman (General Motors)
FM-2 "Wildcat"

The U.S. Navy fighter that finally
was able to match the Japanese
Zero, the Wildcat was not as
agile as its opponent: but tactics,
firepower, and ruggedness
allowed American pilots to meet
the Japanese on equal terms.

Grumman (General Motors) FM-2 "Wildcat"

After takeoff from an aircraft carrier in the Pacific

"This is H. B. Kaltenborn speaking from the NBC Newsroom. It is evident now

that the world, entirely, is at war."

H. B. Kaltenborn, New York, December 8, 1941

Grumman F6F-5K "Hellcat"

The successor to the F4F
Wildcat, the Hellcat was probably
the most important fighter used
by the U.S. Navy. Its victory ratio
over Japanese planes was 19 to 1,
and the Hellcat provided air
superiority in the Pacific during
the war's final years.

USS *Cowpens* at sea, July, 1945

"The President of the United States ordered me to break through the Japanese lines

and proceed from Corregidor to Australia. I came through, and I shall return."

General Douglas MacArthur, Alice Springs, Australia, March 11, 1942

Lt.(jg) Alex Vraciu in his F6F
Hellcat aboard the USS
Lexington a few days after
scoring six victories in eight
minutes during the Marianas
Turkey Shoot, June, 1944

Grumman F6F-3 "Hellcat"

Vought (Goodyear) FG-1D
"Corsair"

Said to be the best carrier-based
fighter of the war, the Corsair
was first used at Guadalcanal in
1943, but the U.S. Navy delayed
its operations on aircraft carriers
until 1944. The Corsair's versa-
tility was demonstrated by
island-based U.S. Marine units.
The Japanese called the Corsair
"Whistling Death."

Short of baseball caps—traditional wear in the South Pacific for Marine airmen—members of Major "Pappy" Boyington's fighter squadron sent a plea to the players in the World Series. Twenty caps soon arrived from the Saint Louis Cardinals, December, 1943.

Vought (Goodyear) FG-1D "Corsair"

Vought (Goodyear)
FG-1D "Corsair"

Ensign Andy Jagger of VF-17
squadron describing an aerial
combat over Rabaul to Lt. H. A.
March, Bougainville, February,
1944

Grumman (General Motors) TBM "Avengers"

At a rear area base in the Pacific, Marine mechanics overhaul Avenger torpedo bombers which have flown patrol missions round-the-clock for a month from Iwo Jima's gutted Motoyama airfield, 1945.

Grumman (General Motors) TBM-3E "Avenger"

Widely acclaimed as the best torpedo bomber of the war, the Avenger first saw action at the Battle of Midway. These aircraft also flew anti-submarine patrols off small escort aircraft carriers in the Atlantic where they helped curtail German U-boat operations.

Douglas SBD-5 (A-24B)
"Dauntless"

"Slow But Deadly," the SBD was obsolete at the beginning of the war but continued to serve well throughout the conflict simply because, despite its lack of power and speed, no other American aircraft offered a performance improvement.

Crew working on Douglas "Dauntless"

Douglas SBD-5 (A-24B) "Dauntless"

Deck crew secures SBD
Dauntless aboard USS
Yorktown, October, 1943.

Curtiss SB2C "Helldiver" returning to
the USS *Hornet*, China Sea, 1945

Curtiss SB2C-5 "Helldiver"

Nicknamed "The Big-tailed
Beast," the Helldiver was less
effective than the Dauntless it
was intended to replace.
Nonetheless, this airplane
served in great numbers with
the American Navy because
dive-bombers were vital in
carrier warfare.

A jungle elephant hauling a
Corsair of the Fleet Air Arm
at an airfield near the Indian
Ocean, 1944

Vought F4U-1A "Corsair"

air

"WHAT's UP DOC"

"Hitler built a fortress around Europe, but he forgot to put a roof on it."
Franklin D. Roosevelt

Curtiss P-40N "Warhawk"

Usually disparaged as not being
a great fighter, the Warhawk
was, nevertheless, produced in
large numbers and was available
in the dark, early days of the
war. Its fame was established
when it equipped the American
Volunteer Group (Flying Tigers)
in China.

A Royal Air Force P-40 is guided
through a Libyan sandstorm by a
crewman, 1942.

An American-built P-40 Kittyhawk undergoes engine tests after arrival at a Royal Air Force maintenance station in the Middle East. Lend-Lease P-40s were sold to the British as the "Kittyhawk" and the "Tomahawk"

"We must be the great arsenal of democracy. For us this is an emergency as serious as war itself."

Franklin D. Roosevelt, fireside chat, December 29, 1940

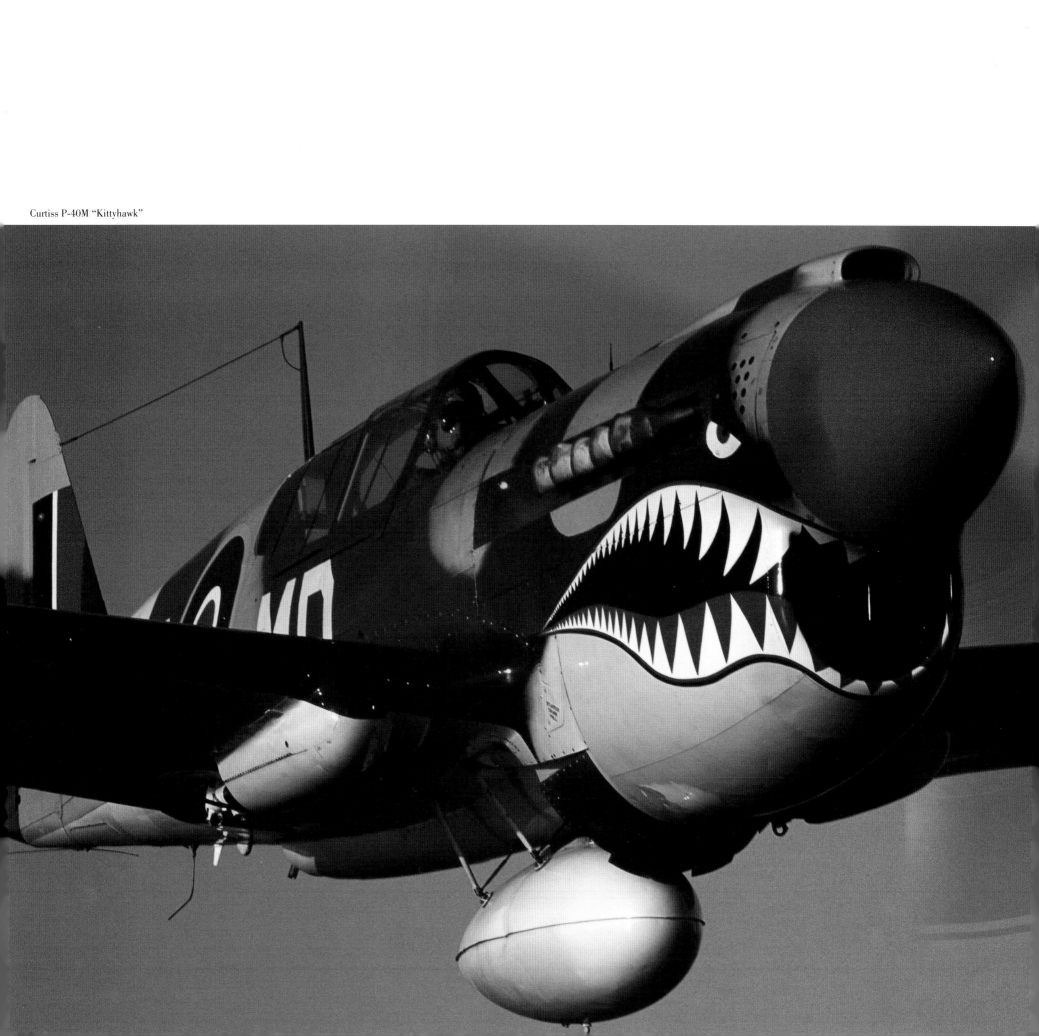

Curtiss P-40E "Warhawk,"
Aleutian Islands, 1943

Curtiss P-40N "Warhawk"

Curtiss P-40K "Warhawk"

Messerschmitt Bf109G-2 Trop

North American P-51D "Mustang"

"Les sanglots longs des violins

de l'automne . . ."

("The long sobs of the autumn violins . . .")

Paul Verlaine, code broadcast from London to
the French Resistance: "The landing will take
place in several days," early June 1944

North American P-51D
"Mustangs"

The best escort fighter of the
war, the Mustang had the long
range capabilities needed to
escort bombers from England
to their targets deep in Europe
and from Iwo Jima to Japan.
Many authorities assert that the
Mustang was the finest all-pur-
pose fighter design of the war.

North American P-51D "Mustang"

North American P-51D
"Mustang"

This Mustang is painted with
black and white "Invasion
Stripes" used to identify Allied
aircraft during the amphibious
landings at Normandy in 1944.

North American
P-51A "Mustang"

"We few, we happy few, we band of brothers;

For he that day that shed his blood with me

Shall be my brother."

William Shakespeare, *Henry V,* Act IV, Scene III

North American P-51D "Mustang"

" . . . blessent mon coeur d'une langueur monotone."

(". . . wound my heart with monotonous languor.")

Paul Verlaine, code broadcast from London to the French Resistance: "The landing will take place in 24 hours," June 5, 1944

North American P-51D "Mustang"

"My friends: Yesterday, June 4, 1944, Rome fell to American and

Allied troops. The first of the Axis capitals is now in our hands.

One up and two to go."

Franklin D. Roosevelt, fireside chat, June 5, 1944

North American P-51D "Mustang"

North American P-51D "Mustang"

A P-47D and aircrew of the 82nd Squadron, 78th Fighter Group, Eighth Air Force based at the Duxford Aerodrome prior to the invasion of Normandy, 1944.

"Soldiers, sailors and airmen of the Allied Expeditionary Force: You are about to embark upon the great crusade toward which we have striven these many months. The eyes of the world are upon you. The hopes and prayers of liberty loving people everywhere march with you. The tide has turned. I have full confidence in your courage, devotion to duty and skill in battle. We will accept nothing less than full victory."

General Dwight D. Eisenhower, Commander, Allied Expeditionary Force, June 5, 1944

Republic P-47D-25-RE "Thunderbolt" over the Duxford Aerodrome

"The battle of France has begun. In the nation, the Empire and the armies,

there is no longer anything but one single hope, the same for all. Behind the

heavy cloud of our blood and our tears is the sun of our grandeur shining

out once again."

Charles de Gaulle, BBC radio broadcast to the French people, June 6, 1944

Republic P-47N "Thunderbolt"

Conceived as a high-altitude interceptor, the "Jug" was also extremely effective as a ground attack airplane and as a long-range escort on bombing missions into Germany. Large, rugged, and fast, it served in all theaters.

"People of western Europe: A landing was made this morning on the coast of France by troops of the Allied

Expeditionary Force. The hour of your liberation is approaching."

General Dwight D. Eisenhower, Commander, Allied Expeditionary Force, June 6, 1944

Lt. Col. Eugene P. Roberts,
Commander, 84th Fighter
Squadron, Duxford, England,
1944

Republic P-47D "Thunderbolt"

"My fellow Americans: Last night, when I spoke with you about the fall of Rome, I knew at that

moment that troops of the United States and our Allies were crossing the Channel in another and

greater operation. It has come to pass with success thus far."

Franklin D. Roosevelt, radio broadcast, June 6, 1944

Douglas C-47 "Skytrain"

Derived from the DC-2 and DC-3 family of commercial airliners, the Skytrain served in every war zone in a wide variety of roles. Robust and dependable, it carried cargo, generals, and paratroopers.

"Almighty God: Our sons, pride of our nation, this day have set upon a mighty endeavor,

a struggle to preserve our republic, our religion, and our civilization, and to set free a

suffering humanity. . . . Help us, Almighty God, to rededicate ourselves in renewed faith

in Thee in this hour of great sacrifice."

Franklin D. Roosevelt, radio broadcast, prayer on the occasion of the Allied Invasion of Europe, June 6, 1944

Douglas C-47-10-DK "Dakota"

Lockheed P-38J "Lightning"

1st Lt. Raymond
S. Cicerone, 1943

Lockheed P-38J "Lightning"

Germans called this airplane *der Gabelschwanz Teufel* (fork-tailed devil). Although big for a fighter, the Lightning was effective. In the Pacific, America's top aces flew Lightnings. In April 1943, a Lightning piloted by Lt. Thomas Lanphier shot down Admiral Yamamoto's plane, killing the Japanese leader.

Lockheed
P-38J-20-LO "Lightning"

Mitsubishi
A6M5-52 Type 0 "Zero"

1st Lt. Lefty Gardner
after receiving the
DFC, 1944

Lockheed
P-38L "Lightning"

Royal Air Force P-39
"Airacobras" of No. 601
Squadron during a press
day at Duxford, England,
October, 1941

Bell P-39Q "Airacobra"

Featuring an engine mounted
behind the pilot, the Airacobra
was outclassed as a fighter early
in the war, but it was widely
used as a ground attack aircraft.
About 4,700 Airacobras were
supplied to Russia, which used
the plane as a tank destroyer.

Bell P-63F "Kingcobra"

A development of the P-39,
the Kingcobra was a superior
airplane that was never used
operationally by the United
States. Under Lend-Lease, it was
supplied in large numbers to
Russia and France as a ground
attack airplane.

Yakolev LET C.11
"Moose"

Three Mikoyan-Gurevich
Mig3 aircraft

"The German troops now resemble a wounded beast which is compelled to crawl back to the frontiers of its lair—Germany—in order to heal its wounds. But a wounded beast does not cease to be a dangerous beast. To rid our country and the countries allied with us from the danger of enslavement, the wounded beast must be pursued close on its heels and finished off in its own lair. Long live our Soviet mother-land! Long live our Red Army and Navy! Long live the great Soviet people! Long live the friendship of the peoples of the Soviet Union! Long live the Soviet men and women guerrillas! Eternal glory to the heroes who fell in the battles for the freedom and independence of our motherland! Death to the German invaders!"

Joseph Stalin, Order of the Day, May 1, 1944

Yakolev LET C.11 "Moose"

Fiat G-59-4B

Douglas A-26C "Invader"

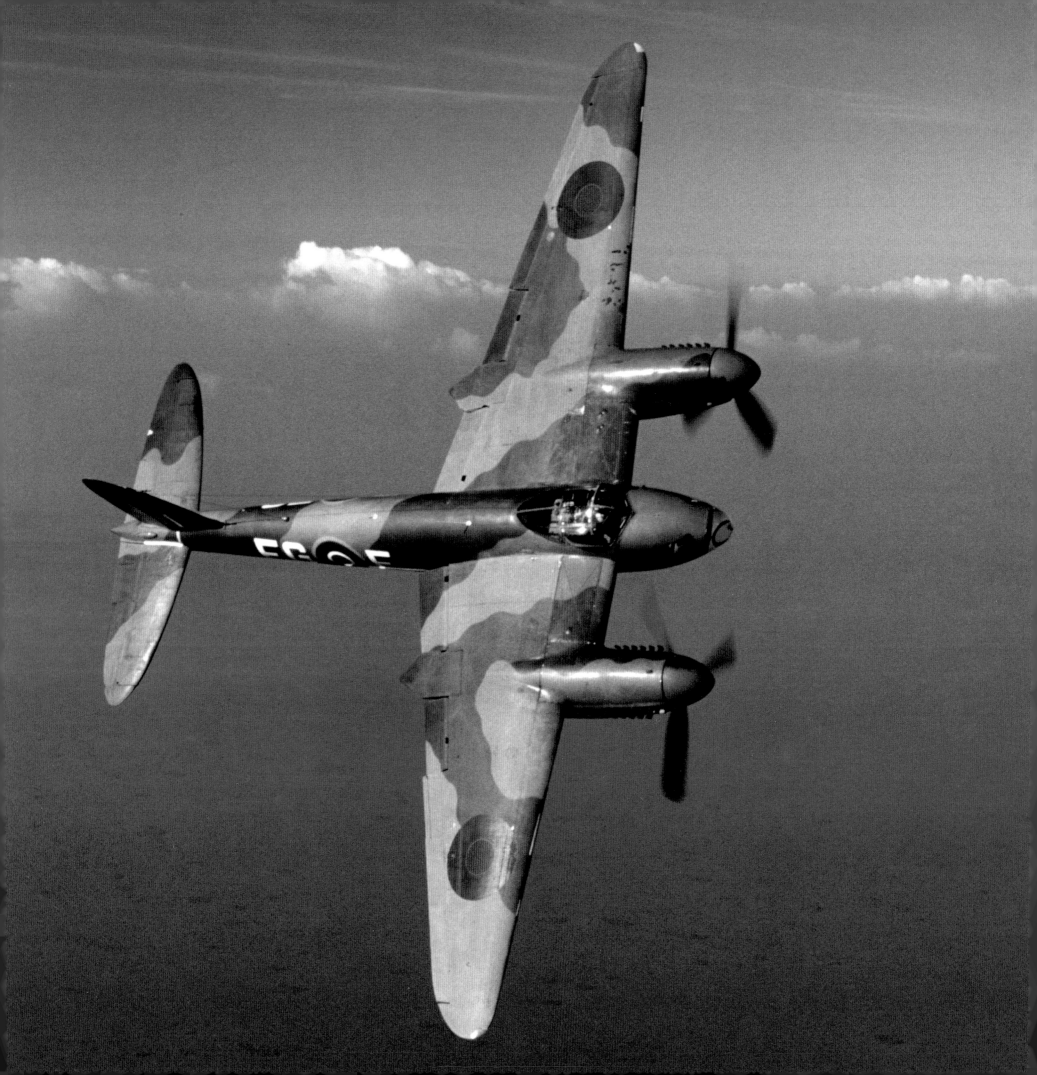

De Havilland B Mk. 35 "Mosquito"

Designed originally as a fast bomber, the Mosquito was soon developed into a potent fighter. Several sections of the plane were constructed of plywood. This popular aircraft was extremely versatile, serving in the fighter, bomber, and photo reconnaissance roles.

A member of the Women's Auxiliary Air Force (WAAF) of the Royal Air Force in Egypt

Avro "Lancaster" B. Mk. X

A product of wartime necessity, the Lancaster was developed in 1941. It has been called the finest British heavy bomber and, by some observers, the finest bomber on either side of the conflict. "Dam-buster" Lancasters conducted the "bouncing bomb" raids that breached two German Ruhr valley river dams.

Avro "Lancaster" B Mk. I

Col. Fred J. Christensen, Jr., 8th Air Force, 1944

"Why should we hide the feelings that fill us all. . . . Paris has risen to free itself with its own hands! Paris! Paris outraged! Paris broken! Paris martyrized! But Paris liberated! Liberated by itself, liberated by its people with the help of the armies of France, with the support and help of the whole of France, of France that is fighting, of France alone!"

Charles de Gaulle, Hotel de Ville, Paris, August 26, 1944

Boeing B-17G "Flying Fortress"

A product of the long pre-war debate in America about the value of strategic bombing, the Flying Fortress became a symbol of America's daylight bombing campaign against Germany.

"*After finally getting over the Hump, we flew over an overcast*

through which we let down into the Yangtze Valley. And there

was China! A most amazing landscape of thousands of cultivated

rice paddies. For the first time in my life I had the feeling of

being in a different world—one that could not be described with

a 'Well, this looks like Texas,' or 'This looks like Iowa.'"

Captain William O'Malley, April 24, 1944

Boeing B-17 "Flying Fortresses" over the Austrian Alps, 1945

Eighth Air Force B-17s of the
452nd Bombardment Group
leave vapor trails over Berlin.

Boeing B-17G "Flying Fortress"

Consolidated B-24J "Liberator"

The Liberator was a mainstay of the United States' bombing operations, not only in Europe but also in Asia. The "Lumbering Lib" was built in greater numbers than any other American warplane.

Col. Charles F. McKenna III,
781st Bomb Squadron,
Pantanella AAB, Italy, 1945

"What kind of a people do they think we are? Is it possible

they do not realize that we shall never cease to persevere

against them until they have been taught a lesson which

they and the world will never forget."

Winston Churchill, address to a Joint Session of the U.S.
Congress

Squadron Ordnance
Crew, 781st Bomb
Squadron, Pantanella
AAB, Italy, 1944

A crew of B-29 mechanics, 1945

"It was the B-29 and the B-29s only that could put tons and tons of bombs on Japan. The fleet couldn't do it; the Naval air couldn't do it; the Army couldn't do it. The B-29s could."

General Henry Harley "Hap" Arnold

Boeing TB-29A "Superfortress"

Continuation of the strategic bombing concept led to the "Superfortress" with its long range, advanced weaponry, and heavy bomb load.

Captured aircraft silhouettes

Grumman F7F-3P "Tigercat"

Supermarine "Spitfire" LF Mk. XVIe

Hawker "Sea Fury" F.B. II

Supermarine "Spitfire" FR Mk. XIV

Royal Air Force "Spitfires"
in the Cocos Islands, 1945

fire

"My Dear Mother, I am an empty dream . . . Like snow left on the mountains in summer. I feel my warm blood moving inside of me And I am reminded that I am living. My soul will have its home in the rising of the sun. If you feel sad, look at the dawn with all of its beauty. You will find me there." The last poem of a kamikaze pilot, a member of the Special Attack Force, Chiran Base, Japan, 1945

"There is no way to describe what a warrior should do other than that he should adhere to the Way of the warrior. By the Way of the warrior is meant Death. It means choosing Death whenever there is a choice between Life and Death. It means nothing more than this."

Yamato Tsunenori, *Ha Gakure*, seventeenth century

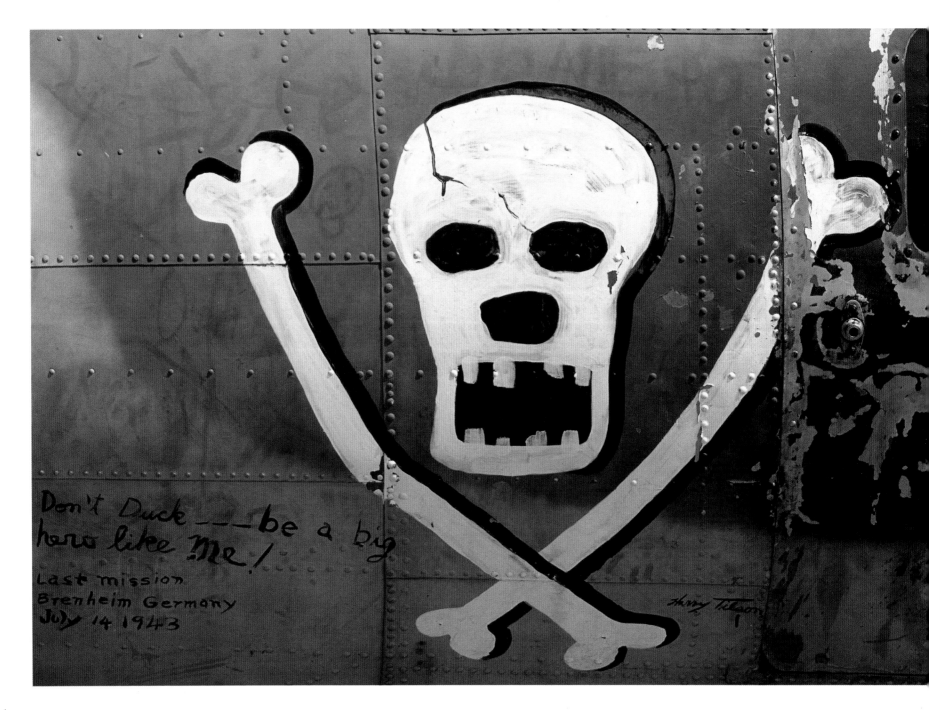

A German V-1 pilotless bomb falls on central London, 1944. 2,350 "Doodlebugs" landed on London, killing 5,475 people and injuring 15,000 others.

Bell P-63 "Kingcobra" firing tracers

"With this signature the German people and the German Armed Forces are, for better or for worse,

delivered into the hands of the victors. . . . In this hour I can only express the hope that the victor will

treat them with generosity."

General Alfred Jodl to General Bedell Smith after signing the unconditional surrender at Reims, May 7, 1945

General Alfred Jodl, Nazi Chief of Staff, disembarks from a USAF C-47 en route to Reims to sign the unconditional surrender, May 6, 1945.

North American P-51D "Mustang"

De Havilland B Mk. 35 "Mosquito"

Captain Ross Messner, bombardier,
after a mission over Germany

"Yesterday morning, at 2:41 A.M. at General Eisenhower's headquarters,

General Jodl, the Representative of the German High Command, and

Grand Admiral Doenitz, the designated head of the German State, signed

the act of unconditional surrender of all German land, sea, and air forces in

Europe to the Allied Expeditionary Force and simultaneously to the Soviet

High Command. We may allow ourselves a brief period of rejoicing."

Winston Churchill, May 8, 1945

Boeing B-17G "Flying Fortress"

Aboard the USS *Saratoga* at dawn

Young pilots, 72nd Shinbu Squadron,
Special Attack Force, 1945

"The year has gone

And so many friends

The lost, the uncounted,

The dead."

Admiral Isoroku Yamamoto,
Commander in Chief, Imperial
Navy, December 7, 1942

A mock aircraft made of bamboo,
Yontan Airfield, Okinawa, 1945

A final gesture of Second Lieutenant Tetsujiro Karasawa, a member of the 57th Shinbu-Tai, Army Special Attack Force, Chiran Base, Kagoshima, Japan, 1945.

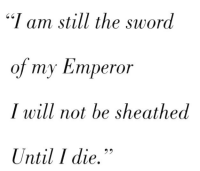

"I am still the sword

of my Emperor

I will not be sheathed

Until I die."

Admiral Isoroku Yamamoto, Commander in Chief, Imperial Navy, haiku written a few days before his death on April 18, 1943

Second Lieutenant Karasawa receiving flowers before his final sortie in a Type 4/Ki-84 Hayate fighter aircraft, Chiran Base, 1945.

Student girls bid farewell to a Special Attack Force pilot, Chiran Base, 1945.

Grumman F6F-5N "Hellcat"

A Japanese aircraft attacking the USS *Sangamon*, May, 1945

Boeing TB-29A "Superfortress"

"At the time of the explosion we were wearing Polaroid welders glasses. They were so dark that even the tropical sun shone through them as nothing more than a vague pinpoint of light. Even then, the explosion, when eventually it came, was so bright that it had the same effect as if night had been turned into day. A few seconds later, when it was safe to take off our glasses, we looked out towards the target and saw a vast ball of fire. It was about 2,000 feet in the air and half a mile in diameter. This fire, which generated almost 10 million degrees of heat, began rocketing up into the heavens at a speed of something like 20,000 feet a minute. After 15 seconds the flame had died out and turned into a cloud. Exactly what that cloud looked like, I do not suppose any words will ever describe. Unlike any other phenomenon the world has ever seen, it was possessed of some diabolical activity, as though it were a horrible form of life. Its heat was so great that even at a range of 20 miles, we could see the dust from the earth being sucked up into the air like a vortex. The cloud rose to a height of 60,000 feet in less than five minutes and there it stayed. On flying close to it we saw that its color was a sort of luminous yellow, like sulfur. Throughout the whole time it remained a boiling, turbulent mass and continued expanding until it reached some two miles across. We knew from what we had been told that its activity would destroy anything that came within its reach."

Group Captain Leonard Cheshire, Nagasaki, Japan, August 9, 1945

Sunrise over a Curtiss SB2C-5 "Helldiver"

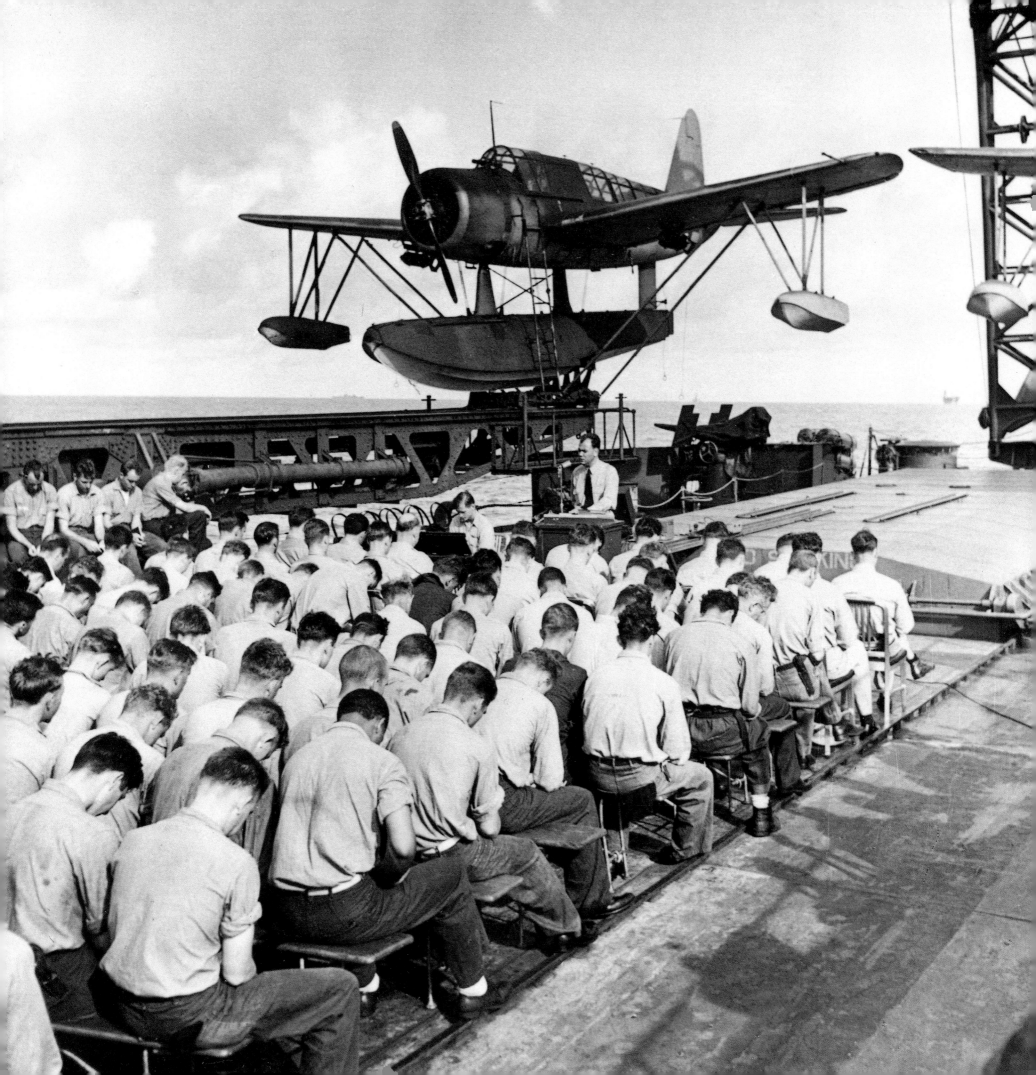

"I have seen war. I have seen war on land and sea. I have seen blood running from the wounded.

I have seen men coughing out their gassed lungs. I have seen the dead in the mud. . . . I have seen

children starving. I have seen the agony of mothers and wives. I hate war."

Franklin D. Roosevelt, Address on the International Situation, Chautauqua, New York, August 14, 1936

North American B-25D
"Mitchell" over the American
Cemetery at Madingley, England,
July, 1993

Aircraft Specifications and Index

Grumman F3F-2, 43

WING SPAN: 32 feet
LENGTH: 23 feet, 2 inches
HEIGHT: 9 feet, 4 inches
POWER: Wright Cyclone R1820-55, 1,050 h.p.
WEIGHT: Empty: 3,254 lbs, Loaded: 4,498 lbs
MAXIMUM SPEED: 260 m.p.h.
SERVICE CEILING: 32,000 feet
RANGE: 975 miles

Grumman F4F-8 "Wildcat" (FM-2), 52–53, 55, 57

WING SPAN: 38 feet
LENGTH: 28 feet, 11 inches
HEIGHT: 11 feet, 5 inches
POWER: One Wright R-1820-56, 1,350 h.p.
WEIGHT: Empty: 5,448 lbs, Loaded: 8,271 lbs
MAXIMUM SPEED: 332 m.p.h.
SERVICE CEILING: 34,700 feet
RANGE: 1,310 miles

Grumman F6F-3 "Hellcat", 54, 57, 59, 148

WING SPAN: 42 feet, 10 inches
LENGTH: 33 feet, 7 inches
HEIGHT: 13 feet, 1 inch
POWER: One Pratt & Whitney R-2800-10W, 2,000 h.p.
WEIGHT: Empty: 9,238 lbs, Loaded: 15,413 lbs
MAXIMUM SPEED: 380 m.p.h.
SERVICE CEILING: 37,300 feet
RANGE: 1,355 miles

Grumman F7F "Tigercat", 130

WING SPAN: 51 feet, 6 inches
LENGTH: 45 feet, 1/2 inch
HEIGHT: 15 feet, 2 inches
POWER: Two Pratt & Whitney R2800-34W Double Wasps, 2,100 h.p. each
WEIGHT: Empty: 16,720 lbs, Loaded: 25,720 lbs
MAXIMUM SPEED: 450 m.p.h
RANGE: 1,800 miles w/external tanks

Grumman F8F-2 "Bearcat", 130–131

WING SPAN: 35 feet, 6 inches
LENGTH: 27 feet, 8 inches
HEIGHT: 12 feet, 2 inches
POWER: One Pratt & Whitney R-2800-34W, 2,300 h.p.
WEIGHT: Empty: 7,690 lbs, Loaded: 13,494 lbs
MAXIMUM SPEED: 447 m.p.h.
SERVICE CEILING: 40,700 feet
RANGE: 1,435 miles

Grumman (General Motors) TBM-3 "Avenger", 66–68

WING SPAN: 54 feet, 2 inches
LENGTH: 40 feet
HEIGHT: 16 feet, 5 inches
POWER: One Wright R-2600-20, 1,900 h.p.
WEIGHT: Empty: 10,843 lbs, Loaded: 18,250 lbs
MAXIMUM SPEED: 267 m.p.h.
SERVICE CEILING: 23,400 feet
RANGE: 2,335 miles

Hawker "Hind", 8

WING SPAN: 37 feet, 3 inches
LENGTH: 29 feet, 7 inches
HEIGHT: 10 feet, 7 inches
POWER: One Rolls Royce Kestrel V, 640 h.p.
WEIGHT: Empty: 3,250 lbs, Loaded: 5,298 lbs
MAXIMUM SPEED: 186 m.p.h.
SERVICE CEILING: 26,400 feet
RANGE: 430 miles

Hawker "Hurricane" Mk. IIB, 7, 16, 25, 37

WING SPAN: 40 feet
LENGTH: 32 feet, 3 inches
HEIGHT: 8 feet, 9 inches
POWER: One Rolls Royce Merlin XX, 1,280 h.p.
WEIGHT: Empty: 5,500 lbs, Loaded: 7,470 lbs
MAXIMUM SPEED: 340 m.p.h.
SERVICE CEILING: 40,000 feet
RANGE: 505 miles

Hawker "Sea Fury", 134

WING SPAN: 38 feet, 4 inches
LENGTH: 34 feet, 7 inches
HEIGHT: 14 feet, 7 1/2 inches
POWER: One Bristol Centaurus 18, 2,480 h.p.
WEIGHT: Empty: 8,700 lbs, Loaded: 11,930 lbs
MAXIMUM SPEED: 445 m.p.h.
SERVICE CEILING: 35,600 feet
RANGE: 1,310 miles

Heinkel He111, 20–21

WING SPAN: 74 feet, 1 1/2 inches
LENGTH: 54 feet, 5 1/2 inches
HEIGHT: 13 feet, 8 inches
POWER: Two Junkers Jumo 211F-2s, 1,340 h.p. each
WEIGHT: Empty: 14,400 lbs, Loaded: 27,400 lbs
MAXIMUM SPEED: 258 m.p.h.
SERVICE CEILING: 25,500 feet
RANGE: 1,740 miles

Junkers Ju52, 12

WING SPAN: 95 feet, 11 1/2 inches
LENGTH: 62 feet
HEIGHT: 18 feet, 2 1/2 inches
POWER: Three BMW 132A-3S, 725 h.p. each
WEIGHT: Empty: 12,610 lbs, Loaded: 23,146 lbs
MAXIMUM SPEED: 172 m.p.h.
SERVICE CEILING: 19,360 feet
RANGE: 620 miles

Junkers Ju87 "Stuka", 22–23

WING SPAN: 45 feet, 3 1/2 inches
LENGTH: 37 feet, 8 3/4 inches
HEIGHT: 12 feet, 9 1/2 inches
POWER: One Junkers Jumo 211J-1, 1,400 h.p.
WEIGHT: Empty: 8,598 lbs, Loaded: 14,550 lbs
MAXIMUM SPEED: 255 m.p.h.
SERVICE CEILING: 23,915 feet
RANGE: 954 miles

Lockheed P-38J "Lightning", 105–106

WING SPAN: 52 feet
LENGTH: 37 feet, 10 inches
HEIGHT: 9 feet, 2 inches
POWER: Two Allison V-1710-89s, 1,425 h.p. each
WEIGHT: Empty: 12,800 lbs, Loaded: 21,600 lbs
MAXIMUM SPEED: 414 m.p.h.
SERVICE CEILING: 44,000 feet
RANGE: 2,600 miles

Martin B-26G "Marauder", 115

WING SPAN: 71 feet
LENGTH: 56 feet, 1 inch
HEIGHT: 20 feet, 4 inches
POWER: Two Pratt & Whitney R-2800-43s, 1,920 h.p. each
WEIGHT: Empty: 25,300 lbs, Loaded: 38,200 lbs
MAXIMUM SPEED: 283 m.p.h.
SERVICE CEILING: 19,800 feet
RANGE: 1,100 miles

Messerschmitt Bf109G-2 Trop, 18–19, 32–33, 86

WING SPAN: 32 feet, 6 1/2 inches
LENGTH: 29 feet, 8 inches
HEIGHT: 8 feet, 6 inches
POWER: One Daimler-Benz DB-605A-1, 1,475 h.p.
WEIGHT: Empty: 5,900 lbs, Loaded: 7,500 lbs
MAXIMUM SPEED: 387 m.p.h.
SERVICE CEILING: 38,500 feet
RANGE: 615 miles

Messerschmitt Me108/Nord 1002 "Taifun", 15

WING SPAN: 34 feet, 5 inches
LENGTH: 27 feet, 2 inches
HEIGHT: 7 feet, 6 1/2 inches
POWER: One AS-10 Renault, 240 h.p.
WEIGHT: Empty: 1,887 lbs, Loaded: 3,087 lbs
MAXIMUM SPEED: 196 m.p.h.
SERVICE CEILING: 15,480 feet
RANGE: 620 miles

Messerschmitt Me208/Nord 1101, 13

WING SPAN: 37 feet, 9 inches
LENGTH: 29 feet
HEIGHT: 11 feet
POWER: One Renault 6Q10A, 240 h.p.
WEIGHT: Empty: 2,426 lbs, Loaded: 3,638 lbs
MAXIMUM SPEED: 193 m.p.h.
SERVICE CEILING: 19,685 feet
RANGE: 753 miles

Mikoyan-Gurevich Mig-3, 110

WING SPAN: 33 feet, 9 1/2 inches
LENGTH: 26 feet, 9 inches
HEIGHT: 11 feet, 6 inches
POWER: One Mikulin AM-35A, 1,350 h.p.
WEIGHT: Empty: 4,500 lbs, Loaded: 7,385 lbs
MAXIMUM SPEED: 407 m.p.h.
SERVICE CEILING: 39,370 feet
RANGE: 510 miles

Mitsubishi A6M5-52 "Zero", 48–49, 106, 139

WING SPAN: 36 feet, 1 inch
LENGTH: 29 feet, 9 inches
HEIGHT: 9 feet, 2 inches
POWER: One Nakajima Sakae 21, 1,130 h.p.
WEIGHT: Empty: 3,920 lbs, Loaded: 6,508 lbs
MAXIMUM SPEED: 358 m.p.h.
SERVICE CEILING: 35,100 feet
RANGE: 1,130 miles

Nakajima Ki-84 "Hayate", 149

WING SPAN: 36 feet, 10 inches
LENGTH: 32 feet, 6 1/2 inches
HEIGHT: 11 feet, 1 1/2 inches
POWER: One Nakajima Ha-45, 1,900 h.p.
WEIGHT: Empty: 5,864 lbs, Loaded: 8,576 lbs
MAXIMUM SPEED: 392 m.p.h.
SERVICE CEILING: 34,350 feet
RANGE: 1,347 miles

Nakajima B5N "Kate", 51

WING SPAN: 50 feet, 11 inches
LENGTH: 33 feet, 10 inches
HEIGHT: 12 feet, 2 inches
POWER: One Sakae 11, 1,000 h.p.
WEIGHT: Empty: 4,830 lbs, Loaded: 8,360 lbs
MAXIMUM SPEED: 235 m.p.h.
SERVICE CEILING: 25,200 feet
RANGE: 1,238 miles

North American B-25D "Mitchell", 113, 154

WING SPAN: 67 feet, 7 inches
LENGTH: 52 feet, 11 inches
HEIGHT: 16 feet, 4 inches
POWER: Two Wright R-2600-13s, 1,700 h.p. each
WEIGHT: Empty: 29,500 lbs, Loaded: 41,800 lbs
MAXIMUM SPEED: 272 m.p.h.
SERVICE CEILING: 25,000 feet
RANGE: 1,275 miles

North American P-51D "Mustang", 87–95, 145

WING SPAN: 37 feet
LENGTH: 32 feet, 3 inches
HEIGHT: 13 feet, 8 inches
POWER: One Packard Merlin V-1650-7, 1,720 h.p.
WEIGHT: Empty: 7,125 lbs, Loaded: 12,100 lbs
MAXIMUM SPEED: 437 m.p.h.
SERVICE CEILING: 41,900 feet
RANGE: 2,300 miles

Republic P-47G "Thunderbolt", 96–99, 101

WING SPAN: 40 feet, 9 inches
LENGTH: 36 feet, 1 inch
HEIGHT: 14 feet, 3 inches
POWER: One Pratt & Whitney R 2800-21, 2,000 h.p. 2,300 h.p. w/ water injection
WEIGHT: Empty: 9,900 lbs, Loaded: 15,000 lbs
MAXIMUM SPEED: 433 m.p.h.
SERVICE CEILING: 42,000 feet
RANGE: 835 miles

Supermarine "Spitfire" Mk. XIV, 24, 135, 160

WING SPAN: 36 feet, 10 inches
LENGTH: 32 feet, 8 inches
HEIGHT: 12 feet, 8 inches
POWER: One Rolls Royce Griffon 65, 2,050 h.p.
WEIGHT: Empty: 6,700 lbs, Loaded: 10,280 lbs
MAXIMUM SPEED: 448 m.p.h.
SERVICE CEILING: 43,000 feet
RANGE: 460 miles

Supermarine "Spitfire" Mk. XVI, 17, 24, 29, 35, 39, 133–137

WING SPAN: 36 feet, 10 inches
LENGTH: 31 feet, 4 inches
HEIGHT: 11 feet, 5 inches
POWER: One Rolls Royce "Merlin 266", 1,705 h.p.
WEIGHT: Empty: 5,800 lbs, Loaded: 7,500 lbs
MAXIMUM SPEED: 420 m.p.h.
SERVICE CEILING: 42,500 feet
RANGE: 434 miles

Vought (Goodyear) FG-1D (F4U) "Corsair", 60–61, 63–65, 74–75

WING SPAN: 41 feet
LENGTH: 34 feet, 6 inches
HEIGHT: 14 feet, 9 inches
POWER: One Pratt & Whitney R-2800, 2,300 h.p.
WEIGHT: Empty: 9,683 lbs, Loaded: 14,106 lbs
MAXIMUM SPEED: 470 m.p.h.
SERVICE CEILING: 41,600 feet
RANGE: 1,120 miles

Vought-Sikorsky OS2U-3 "Kingfisher", 46

WING SPAN: 35 feet, 11 inches
LENGTH: 33 feet, 10 inches
HEIGHT: 15 feet, 1 1/2 inches
POWER: One Pratt & Whitney R-985-AN-2, 450 h.p.
WEIGHT: Empty: 4,123 lbs, Loaded: 6,000 lbs
MAXIMUM SPEED: 164 m.p.h.
SERVICE CEILING: 13,000 feet
RANGE: 805 miles

Yakolev LET C.11"Moose", 110–111

WING SPAN: 30 feet, 10 inches
LENGTH: 27 feet, 11 inches
HEIGHT: 10 feet, 9 inches
POWER: One Svetsov ASh-21, 570 h.p.
WEIGHT: Empty: 4,190 lbs, Loaded: 5,290 lbs
MAXIMUM SPEED: 295 m.p.h.
SERVICE CEILING: 23,290 feet
RANGE: 795 miles

Aircraft Photo Credits

Chapter 1: Cornwall, England; Hawker "Hurricane" Mk. II

Chapter 2: Pacific Ocean near San Francisco; Grumman J2F-6 "Duck"

Chapter 3: Clouds; North American F-51 "Mustang"

Chapter 4: Sunrise, Wanaka, New Zealand; Mitsubishi A6M5-52 "Zero"

Historical Index

Historical Photo Credits

Diving with a Supermarine
"Spitfire" FR Mk. XIV toward
Mount Aspiring near Wanaka,
New Zealand, April 4, 1994

Acknowledgments

Thanks go to The American Air Museum in Britain,
The Confederate Air Force, The Fighter Collection,
The Lone Star Flight Museum, The Old Flying Machine Company,
The Imperial War Museum, The Battle of Britain Memorial Flight,
The Royal Navy Historic Flight, The Planes of Fame Air Museum,
The Breckenridge Air Museum, The Canadian Warplane Heritage,
Historic Flying Limited, The Shuttleworth Collection,
The Alpine Fighter Collection, The Weeks Air Museum,
The New Zealand Warbirds Association, Aerotec Pty. Ltd.,
The Kalamazoo Aviation History Museum, Queensland Warbirds,
Air World, The Collings Foundation, Planes of Fame East,
The Gathering of Warbirds, Madera and
The Reno Air Races Association.

Special thanks to the brilliant pilots of our photo aircraft:
Captain Larry Daudt, Charles Hutchins, Eddie van Fossen,
Al Goss, Jimmie Ruel McMillan, Mike "Chico" Burke, Bill Arnot,
Nelson Ezell, Ralph Royce, L. Jay Cullum, Alan Bush, Steve Hinton,
John Romain, Sue Parish, Kevin Eldridge, and Denny Ghiringhelli.

And thanks to Marshall P. Cloyd, Edward Inman, Colonel Lloyd Nolen,
Colonel Lefty Gardner, Howard Pardue, Stephen Grey, Hoof Proudfoot,
Ray Hanna, Mark Hanna, Tim Wallis, Kermit Weeks, Lt. Cmdr. John Beattie,
Sqdn. Ldr. Andy M. Tomalin, Group Capt. Andy Williams, Robert L. Waltrip,
Ralph Royce, Jim Fausz, Robert J. Pond, Ronnie Gardner, Ruby Gardner,
Reg Urschler, Tom Cloyd, Mike Collier, Bob Ayars, Bill Crump,
Tom Gregory, Lt. Cmdr. Dave Knight, John Lamont, Lindsay Walton,
E.K. Coventry, Charlie Brown, Clive Denny, Tim Routsis, Angus McVitie,
BEA Lewis, Paul Bonhomme, Nick Grey, Russ Snadden, Dave Southwood,
Graham Warner, Sarah Hanna, Keith Skilling, Tom Middleton, Ray Mulqueen,
Guido Zuccoli, Tony Chamberlain, Wayne Milburn, Rob Booth, Qwilton Biel,
Eddie Doherty, Paul Radley, John Rayner, Ed Maloney, John Maloney,
Karen Hinton, Joe Haley, Jerry Wilkins, John Crocker, Bill Destefani,
David Price, William Clark, Sherman Smoot, Harold Kinsvater, Mike DeMarino,
Stewart Brickenden, Don Fisher, Cy Dunbar, Dennis Bradley, Pete Parish,
Bob Ellis, John Ellis, John Hess, Greg Klassen, Larry Klassen, Jean Garric,
Nicole Garric, Bill Parker, Ron Hevle, Fred Sebby, Wally McDonald,
Merrill Wien, Ross Grady, Walter Wooton, Aubrey Hair, Jim Williams,
Gary Meermans, Kay Meermans, John Paul, Wilbur West, Harold Zook,
Art McKinley, W.L. Bryan, Elmer Ward, Mike Wells, Bob Thompson,
Alex Vraciu, Colette Byatt, Pippa Vaughn, David Henchie, Robert Nishimura,
Jean Makanna, Christie Makanna, Tiffany Doesken, Greg Polos, Davie Blades,
Drew Montgomery, and Chuck Robbins.